Is Social Media Good for Society?

Andrea C. Nakaya

San Diego, CA

© 2017 ReferencePoint Press, Inc.
Printed in the United States

For more information, contact:
ReferencePoint Press, Inc.
PO Box 27779
San Diego, CA 92198
www. ReferencePointPress.com

LIBRARY OF CONGRESS CATALOGING-IN-PUBLICATION DATA

Names: Nakaya, Andrea C., 1976- author.
Title: Is social media good for society? / by Andrea C. Nakaya.
Description: San Diego, CA : ReferencePoint Press, Inc., 2017. | Series:
  Issues in society | Includes bibliographical references and index.
Identifiers: LCCN 2016022846 (print) | LCCN 2016027304 (ebook) | ISBN
  9781682820681 (hardback) | ISBN 9781682820698 (eBook)
Subjects: LCSH: Social media--Juvenile literature. | Online social
  networks--Juvenile literature. | Internet--Social aspects--Juvenile literature.
Classification: LCC HM742 .N348 2017 (print) | LCC HM742 (ebook) | DDC
  302.23/1--dc23
LC record available at https://lccn.loc.gov/2016022846

CONTENTS

An Essential Part of Life

In 2015 US astronaut Scott Kelly was preparing to go into space, where he planned to live for a record-breaking twelve months. In a State of the Union address, President Barack Obama recognized Kelly's upcoming voyage, then added, "Make sure to Instagram it."[1] Kelly did use social media such as Instagram and Twitter to document and share his time in space. As *Boston Globe* writer Heather Ciras states:

> To say he's delivered is a bit of an understatement: Kelly posted about 750 images while in space for 340 days. He spearheaded the hashtags #YearInSpace and #EarthArt, and helped promote NASA's campaign #WhySpaceMatters. He sent a #GoodnightFromSpace photo nearly every night, showed us the flowers he grew aboard the International Space Station, commented on weather patterns, posted what our cities look like from space, and sent video of himself in a gorilla suit chasing a fellow astronaut.[2]

Social media has become an integral part of life for the majority of Americans and for many people around the world. While not everyone has the opportunity to share experiences as unique as Kelly's, it is not unusual for people to be just as active on social media.

A New Way to Communicate

Research shows that about two-thirds to three-quarters of Americans use social media, and that number increases every year. People go online to talk to their friends, share photos and videos, play social games, look for dates, find jobs, see where their friends are, get news and information, and do many other things. In 2014 the *Wall Street Journal* published a report on social media by research company Gallup that shows that Americans spend a significant amount of time using social media. The report says:

The statistics surrounding social media are dizzying. Consider that in just one day:

- Facebook users post 4.75 billion items of content
- Twitter users send 400 million tweets
- Instagram users "like" 1.2 billion photos
- YouTube users watch 4 billion videos.[3]

The Pew Research Center, which has also conducted numerous research studies about how and why Americans use social media, concludes, "Social media networks have become vital channels for Americans' daily interactions."[4] As smartphones have proliferated, many people have begun to access their account through their phones, meaning that they are often constantly connected to their networks.

Astronaut Scott Kelly, shown here juggling fresh fruit aboard the International Space Station, proved to be an avid user of social media. Kelly reportedly posted approximately 750 photos during his year in orbit.

Social media is so integral to life that it has dramatically changed the way people interact and communicate with one another. In the past, the majority of social interaction occurred face-to-face or over the phone. James P. Steyer, founder and chief executive officer (CEO) of Common Sense Media, believes that social media is taking the place of that type of interaction. He says, "It's displacing and replacing the real, physical world of interaction and communication that's always been the core human experience."[5] Instead, he observes that many people carry out a vast amount of their social lives entirely on social networks. With the rise in popularity of social networks as a way to communicate, it is common to hear people say that they actually dislike talking in person or over the phone. For example, Amy Pickworth, an editor at the Rhode Island School of Design, explains that a phone call takes too much of her time. "Even if it's someone I know well and love, I resent the intrusion," she explains. "The phone is so pushy. It's just suddenly so *there*, demanding, 'Talk to me, say funny things,' or 'I'm sad, cheer me up,' or 'Holy cow, listen to this.'"[6] Many people prefer social media conversations because they can engage in them in their own time and on their own terms.

> "[Social media is] displacing and replacing the real, physical world of interaction and communication that's always been the core human experience."[5]
>
> —James P. Steyer is the founder and CEO of Common Sense Media.

An Unknown Future

The takeover of social media has happened very quickly. Statistics portal Statista estimates that from 2010 to 2015, the number of social media users worldwide more than doubled, from 970 million to 2.04 billion. It predicts that users will reach 2.72 billion by 2019. US data shows a similarly rapid increase. The Pew Research Center reports that in 2015, 76 percent of adult Internet users in the United States used social networking sites, while in 2005 only 8 percent did. As these data reveal, ten years ago, social media was something few people did, but it has quickly become difficult to imagine life without it.

Because social networking has flourished so quickly, nobody is sure how it will affect society in the future. There has simply not been enough time to see the long-term effects of social media. In addition, social media use continues to evolve and change, making it even more difficult to understand and predict its effects. Overall, there remains fierce debate over whether social media is good for society. Good or bad though, there is no doubt that social media is affecting the world. Steyer warns that society should not ignore its importance. He says, "Make no mistake. This is a huge change that's occurring at warp speed."[7]

1 What Are the Facts?

The Pew Research Center is a nonpartisan organization that conducts research about numerous issues and trends that are important in the United States. It has been tracking social media use since 2005, so it has more than ten years of data about social media trends. The organization finds that in those ten years social networking has changed from a relatively rare activity to something that the majority of Americans engage in. In 2005 it found that just 7 percent of US adults used social media, while by 2015 that number had reached 65 percent. Social media has become an integral part of life for most Americans and for a growing number of people around the world, and most experts believe its presence will only increase in the future.

Popular Social Media

Social media includes websites and applications that let users join online communities, where they can create and share various types of content with other members of the community. The most common reason people use social media is to connect with friends and family, and sites such as Facebook and Snapchat facilitate that through activities such as status updates, games, and photo sharing. Some social media sites are more specialized, focusing on specific types of content. For example, there are numerous sites based on the concept of sharing music, photos, or videos. YouTube—with more than 1 billion users—is one of the most popular, and it allows people to watch and share videos. Instagram is another popular site, where users primarily share photos. Other social media sites are based on connecting people with certain types of shared interests. For example, LinkedIn is a popular site for finding a new job or networking within a person's career field. Dating websites like Zoosk let people find and connect with potential matches. Another popular type of social media is microblogging. Microblog sites only allow short posts; for example, Twitter restricts posts to 140 characters. Microblogging sites like Twitter are usually more public, with users often trying to broadcast their content to as many people as possible.

Facebook is the world's most popular social media site, and it grows larger every day. In 2012 it became the first site to reach 1 billion users. In 2015 cofounder Mark Zuckerberg announced that the site had reached another record, with more than 1 billion people using it in just a single day. In the United States Facebook is the most popular social networking site, with 71 percent of online Americans having an account, according to the Pew Research Center. The social media agency We Are Social maintains that Facebook shows no signs of losing its dominance. In fact, in early 2016 the agency reported, "Facebook is still adding around half a million new users every day, or almost 6 new users *every second*."[8] By mid-2016 Facebook had more than 1.5 billion users.

While Facebook dominates overall, there are hundreds of other social media sites, and many of them also have a large number of members. The statistics portal Statista reports that after Facebook, the most popular social media sites worldwide are WhatsApp, Facebook Messenger, QQ, WeChat, QZone, Tumblr, Instagram, and Twitter. In 2015 research company comScore reported on the most popular social networks in the United States. It found that after Facebook, Google+ is second, used by 38 percent of the online US population. After Google+ are LinkedIn (37 percent), Twitter (36 percent), Instagram (34 percent), Pinterest (29 percent), and Tumblr (25 percent).

In some countries, the government controls and restricts Internet content, and as a result, some of the most popular social networks are banned. For example, Facebook, Twitter, Instagram, Blogger, and a number of other sites are banned in China. Instead, QZone and WeChat are the most popular sites there. Pakistan, Turkey, North Korea, and Iran have all instituted various types of blocks on social media to wall their citizens off from the outside world. However, people in most of these countries often find ways to get around the bans. Only North Korea has isolated its citizens completely by barring Internet service providers.

Facebook has become the world's most popular social networking site. In 2012 it became the first site to reach 1 billion users worldwide.

Social Media Demographics

In the United States research shows that the majority of adults and teens use social media. For instance, in 2016 Statista found that more than three-quarters of Americans had a social network profile. In 2015 the Pew Research Center studied social media to see how it was used by different age groups. The organization found that young adults ages eighteen to twenty-nine are the heaviest users, with 90 percent of them reporting that they use social media. Teens are also very likely to use social media; 76 percent of those ages thirteen to seventeen do so. At just 35 percent, seniors are much less likely to use social media; however, Pew reports that this percentage has been rapidly increasing in recent years. While it did find notable differences in use by age, the organization reports that approximately the same percentage of men and women use social networks. It also

"People in the U.S. check their Facebook, Twitter, and other social media accounts a staggering 17 times a day."[10]

—Lulu Chang is a writer for Digital Trends.

finds that there are no notable racial or ethnic differences for usage in the United States.

Social media use is also popular in the rest of the world. According to We Are Social, in 2016 almost a third of the world's population used social media, or about 2.31 billion people. The agency finds that North and South America have a high rate of usage, while use in Central and South Asia is much lower. It also reports specifically on some of the countries with the highest and lowest use:

> When it comes to individual countries, Taiwan achieves this year's "most social" award, with 77% of the total population using Facebook in the past 30 days. South Korea comes in at number two, with 38.4 million of its total 50.4 million population using KakaoTalk each month. At the low end of the scale, North Korea comes in last place again, with just 6,800 users out of a total population of more than 25 million. However, this is probably unsurprising given that there are no internet services providers in the reclusive North-Asian state. Turkmenistan comes in second-to-last place, registering just 0.2% for social media use.[9]

As Internet access penetrates further throughout the world every year, these percentages are all likely to increase.

Not only do millions of people use social media, but many spend large amounts of their time doing so. Research company Informate Mobile Intelligence investigated social media use around the world. The company found that social media use is significant, says Digital Trends writer Lulu Chang. She explains:

> People in the U.S. check their Facebook, Twitter, and other social media accounts a staggering 17 times a day, meaning at least once every waking hour, if not more. But Americans aren't even the most dependent on these networks when compared to denizens of other countries—in fact, smartphone users in Thailand, Argentina, Malaysia, Qatar, Mexico, and South Africa checked these networking apps at least 40 times a day.[10]

Social Media Algorithms

On some social media sites, the posts that appear in users' feeds are not simply a chronological list of their friends' activity. Instead, some sites filter feeds using complex algorithms. These algorithms personalize what a user sees according to factors such as whether he or she has interacted with or hidden this type of post before or how popular the post is with other people. One reason for filtering social media feeds is to make them more engaging to users. Journalist Megan Anderle explains that while it is known that algorithms are used on some sites, the exact nature of these algorithms is unknown. She says:

> Algorithms are a mystery to researchers. Considered trade secrets, algorithms are best kept confidential. Researchers have a general understanding of how they work, but algorithms are constantly changing so that companies maintain a competitive advantage. Researchers have no way of knowing for sure exactly how Google, Facebook, Twitter, Instagram or any other online platform's algorithms work.

> Many people do not even realize that what they see is being filtered. In 2013 University of Illinois Urbana-Champaign researcher Karrie Karahalios investigated how people change their online behavior as a result of such algorithms. She found that many people were surprised to learn that algorithms are used. "We got a lot of visceral responses to the discovery when they didn't know," she says. "A lot of people just spent literally five minutes being in shock."

Megan Anderle, "How Facebook and Google's Algorithms Are Affecting Our Political Viewpoints," *Huffington Post*, October 15, 2015. www.huffingtonpost.com.

Quoted in Victor Luckerson, "Here's How Facebook's News Feed Actually Works," *Time*, July 9, 2015. www.time.com.

Smartphones have made it much easier to spend a lot of time using social media, because they allow people to access their social media accounts whenever they want to. Researchers believe that as smartphones become more widespread, social media time will continue to increase.

Teens and Social Media

A number of studies have focused specifically on how young people use social media, and there is evidence that teens spend a significant amount of time networking. For example, in 2015 Common Sense Media surveyed 2,658 US children ages eight to eighteen and found that while social media use is minimal among younger children, it is an important part of many teens' day. The researchers report that while tweens spend only about sixteen minutes per day on social media, teens spend an average of one hour and eleven minutes every day. Ten percent of those teens surveyed spend more than three hours a day social networking. Researchers found that teen girls generally spend more time than boys do networking—about forty minutes more per day. They conclude, "There is no question that social media have become an integral part of most teens' lives."[11] The Pew Research Center has also studied social media use by teens and reports that the most popular site among teens is Facebook, used by 71 percent of thirteen- to seventeen-years-olds. The typical user has 145 Facebook friends. Fifty-two percent of teens said they use Instagram, 41 percent said they use Snapchat, and 33 percent use Twitter. Overall, the majority said they use more than one social networking site.

Some research has shown that although teens use social media to socialize, they are also likely to spend a significant amount of time on these sites just looking at content posted by other people. CNN researchers observed the social media use of more than two hundred thirteen-year-olds across the United States in order to understand what they are doing on social media. The researchers report, "Adolescents are spending vast amounts of time just 'lurking,' reading the never-ending stream of their peers' activities without posting anything themselves."[12] The researchers found that more than a third of those studied check social media twenty-five times or more on weekend days, without posting anything. Some users said that they check their social

> "There is no question that social media have become an integral part of most teens' lives."[11]
>
> —Common Sense Media is an organization that works to educate families about safe media use.

media accounts more than one hundred times a day, including while they are in classes at school.

However, while there is evidence that social networking is generally very important to teens, some researchers point out that many teens spend just as much time engaging in other types of entertainment, such as listening to music. In the Common Sense Media survey, researchers found that while social networking has become extremely popular, it actually still lags behind a number of other entertainment activities. The researchers state, "For a generation often defined by its use of social media, it is interesting that it doesn't get the same devotion that listening to music or watching TV do. A significant number of teens say they use social media 'every day' (45 percent), but that's far less than the proportion that listens to music (66 percent) or watches TV (58 percent) that often."[13] In fact, say the researchers, on an average day, 42 percent of teens do not use social media at all.

A teenager uses his smartphone while sitting in class. Researchers have found that use of social media can be distracting for students.

Social Media and Current Events

In addition to providing a way to keep up with friends, social media has become important to news and politics. There has been a dramatic increase in the number of people who say they follow politics or get news about current events on social media. For example, according to a 2016 survey by the Media Insight Project, an initiative of the American Press Institute and the Associated Press-NORC Center for Public Affairs Research, 51 percent of Americans get their news from social networks. Eighty-seven percent of them say they get it on Facebook. YouTube, Twitter, and Instagram are the next most popular sites. The Pew Research Center reports that it has becoming increasingly popular to follow political figures on social media. It says that since 2010 the number of registered voters who follow politicians has doubled. Many people say that social media is actually their preferred source for news because they can personalize the information they receive and because social media feeds provide them with the most up-to-date information possible.

> "Social media has become popular because it lacks the central control of information found in a one-way traditional media communication system. No longer do politicians and the media control the dialogue."[14]
>
> —Mark Fidelman is a contributor for *Forbes.*

Getting news and political information via social media is different than getting it from the television or newspaper because users have more control over what they read or view. *Forbes* contributor Mark Fidelman explains that before the rise of social media, the dissemination of news was controlled by large media companies, and those companies chose what news to broadcast. However, he says that the use of social media has changed things because it allows anyone with a social media account to share information. He maintains, "Social media has become popular because it lacks the central control of information found in a one-way traditional media communication system. No longer do politicians and the media control the dialogue."[14]

Social Media Mining

While conversations about social media often focus on how members use their accounts, social media accounts are also used by companies. All the activity on social media sites creates massive amounts of data about the preferences and opinions of users, and many companies can use that data to make money. For example, one of the most common uses of opinion and preference data is for advertising. Social media sites contain a lot of information about the likes, dislike, habits, and activities of their members, and by analyzing this data, advertisers are able to create more effective advertising. Many social networks sell user data to advertisers. Third-party applications on social media also mine data about users for advertising, research, or other purposes. A

A young woman reads a newspaper. Users of social media have more control over what they read or view than those who use traditional types of mass media.

Social Media in the Classroom

An increasing number of schools are beginning to utilize social media as an educational tool. Some teachers use it as a forum for discussion and collaboration. For example, teacher Brianna Crowley explains that her students use Instagram, Twitter, Flickr, Skype, and blogging to publish their writing for others to read. She says, "Social media provides venues for students to share their stories both within and beyond the classroom." Others teachers use it as a way to engage students by providing a unique type of learning experience. For instance, in Massachusetts teacher Kader Adjout's history class, students use social media to learn about history firsthand by talking to students in other countries. Adjout insists, "You can't find this in a textbook." However, despite increasing interest, teachers who use social media in the classroom remain in the minority. In 2015 a University of Phoenix College of Education survey was conducted by Harris Poll. Of the 1,002 US K-12 teachers who were surveyed, only 13 percent reported that they have integrated social media into the classroom. Researchers found that a primary reason for such a low level of use is that teachers lack training in how to use this technology.

Brianna Crowley, "Connecting a Classroom: Reflections on Using Social Media with My Students," *Education Week Teacher*, September 9, 2015. www.edweek.org.

Kader Adjout, "Social Media Goes to School," *Scholastic*, Winter 2014. www.scholastic.com.

third-party application is a program that is not actually part of the social network but interacts with it; for example, a game or quiz. In many cases social media users are not aware that their data is being used; however, by agreeing to use a social media site or third-party application, a user is typically agreeing to let that application access his or her profile information.

In addition to advertisers and third-party applications, many other individuals, businesses, and institutions are interested in the wealth of personal data that can be found on social media. Some use social media as a research tool. According to the Privacy Rights Clearinghouse, there is evidence that government agencies, law enforcement, and creditors also look at social networking sites in order to get more information about people. For example, employers might research job applicants on social media, or lenders might use social media to help determine a borrower's creditworthiness. Some intrusions, though, are more sinister. For example, identity thieves and scam artists can use personal information for criminal purposes such as hijacking credit cards or opening lines of credit. Stalkers and bullies can use it to harass people. The Federal Bureau of Investigation says:

> Criminals who troll social networking sites looking for information or people to target for exploitation run the gamut— from sexual predators, hackers, and financial fraudsters to business competitors and foreign state actors. . . . Once in the hands of criminals, this personal information can be used to conduct all kinds of cyber attacks against you or your family members, friends, or business associates.[15]

While individuals are often unhappy to realize that their personal information is being used in ways other than they intend, because social networks are still relatively new, there are currently few laws in the United States to protect users' data.

"Criminals who troll social networking sites looking for information or people to target for exploitation run the gamut—from sexual predators, hackers, and financial fraudsters to business competitors and foreign state actors."[15]

—The Federal Bureau of Investigation.

A Part of the Future

Despite the potential risks, social media continues to grow in popularity. In 2014 news organization CNBC asked a number of experts where they think social media will be in twenty-five years, and many predicted that it will become completely integrated into daily life. For example, digital strategist and editor at National Public Radio Melody Kramer says, "It will become part of the fabric of our clothes, part of the glasses we wear and the shoes we put on, and the gadgets we no longer see as gadgets but as part of our very selves. . . . It won't require any effort on our part to share any part of our lives."[16] Whether or not social media becomes fully integrated into people's lives, most experts agree that it will remain a very important part of society in the future.

In a post on the website Social Media Week, teenager Sophie Laing explains how she uses social media. First, she stresses that it is a critical part of her social life. She insists, "For my generation, using social media is fundamental for how we communicate day-to-day with each other." Laing says that she uses five or six different social media sites and apps daily. Her favorite is Snapchat, and she explains how she uses it:

> In my head, the process starts with seeing something cool, snapping a quick photo or video, adding a caption, and sending to my Snapchat friends. It's just about as real-time as it gets too, and my friends can instantly see what I'm doing in that exact moment. And usually, my friends will reply with a photo and caption, and I get to see what *they're doing* as well. Photos and videos on Snapchat are no longer than 10 seconds, and it's this short, ephemeral, close-to-real-life sharing that really sparks my interest, and quite frankly, a lot of my time."[17]

Laing also uses WhatsApp, Facebook, Twitter, Instagram, and StumbleUpon. Like Laing, many people report that social media is an important part of how they interact with others; however, there is debate over how this reliance has affected social dynamics. Some people see no problem with using social media for hours a day, while others contend that this form of communication has some negative effects.

Connecting with Others

Advocates insist that social networks are beneficial because they facilitate and enhance connection between people. The majority of users say that social connection is their main reason for using social media. For example, according to a 2014 report on social media by research company Gallup, published in the *Wall Street*

Journal, 94 percent of those using social media do so to connect with friends and family. Social media makes connecting easy. For example, a person can share news about his or her life with hundreds of people in one easy post, whereas doing so over the phone or in person might take hours. Social media also makes it much easier to keep in contact with friends and family who live in different cities or countries and are therefore difficult to see in person on a regular basis. Many people report that their relationships are stronger as a result of regular interaction through social media. Kim Garst, who writes for social media marketing firm Boom Social, found this after she posted a Facebook message asking for stories of how social media has made a difference in people's lives. For instance, Amanda Brazel responded by explaining how social media has made her closer to her cousin. She says, "He is the only family I am really close to and we've never met in person . . . yet. He lives in Alaska and I in NC. We share pictures of our kids, videos and more. We text each other everyday now. He means so much to me . . . like the brother I never had! Thank you Facebook."[18] Others echoed Brazel's sentiments, insisting that social media helps maintain social connections and builds strong relationships.

Social media also makes it much easier for users to connect with others who share similar interests. There are thousands of different social media groups based on all kinds of unique special interests. For example, Last.fm is a site that allows musicians and music lovers to listen to music and connect with one another, DateMyPet is a dating site for pet lovers, and REMcloud allows members to share their dreams with one another. *Forbes* contributor Drew Hendricks insists that without social media, it would be much more difficult for members of many of these groups to find others who share their interests. He says, "It's the only way many people could ever communicate with each other, removing barriers of geography, time zones, societal restraints, and cultural habits—leaving them only with their common ideas and passions."[19] In online posts, members of Goodreads—a social network site that allows authors and readers to share book reviews and recommendations—are enthusiastic about the connections

A girl poses for a selfie with her dog. Many users of social media say that sharing photos and short videos is an important means of communicating with friends.

they make on the site. One says, "When you finish a great book you feel excited and want to share it with the world and 'here' is where we get to do it."[20] Another comments, "I found wonderful people here and who share a love of reading. It's a pleasure to be part of this great community that loves books."[21]

The Desire to Be Social

Some experts argue that social networks actually fulfill a critical social role because they help satisfy the innate human desire to be social. Author and keynote speaker Dennis Merritt Jones explains, "Every person desires someone to witness their life. People want to know that who they are matters and that their presence on the planet makes a difference. Who among us does not long to be acknowledged, appreciated, well-received and supported by others?"[22] Jones and others believe that social media sites are so popular because they help people make this connection with others.

Researcher Danah Boyd has spent years researching the role of social media in young people's lives, and she argues that its role in facilitating socialization is particularly important to this age group. She explains that in recent years it has become more difficult for young people to socialize in person. The reasons for this difficulty include busy schedules, protective parents, living too far away from one another, going to different schools, and not being old enough to drive or not having a car. As a result, Boyd finds that many young people have turned to social media. She says:

> The social media tools that teens use are direct descendants of the hangouts and other public places in which teens have been congregating for decades. What the drive-in was to teens in the 1950s and the mall in the 1980s, Facebook, texting, Twitter, instant messaging, and other social media are to teens now. Teens flock to them knowing they can socialize with friends and become better acquainted with classmates and peers they don't know as well. . . . Teens want to gossip, flirt, complain, compare notes, share passions, emote, and joke around. They want to be able to talk among themselves.[23]

Boyd says that during her research, young people repeatedly told her that they would much rather meet in person, but that was often impossible, so they use social media instead.

Disagreement over How Many Friends a Person Can Have

Social networks make it so easy to create and maintain friendships that it is not uncommon for members to have hundreds of friends. However, critics argue that while it might be possible to network with hundreds of people, many of these friendships end up being superficial because it is simply not possible to have hundreds of true friends. Psychologist Robin Dunbar has conducted extensive research on social dynamics and believes that most humans are not able to have more than 150 meaningful relationships. He says, "The figure of 150 seems to represent the maximum number of individuals with whom we can have a genuinely social relationship, the kind of relationship that goes with knowing who they are and how they relate to us."[24] He explains that this is because it takes work to maintain meaningful relationships, and people are only capable of doing so much work. "The amount of social capital you have is pretty fixed," says Dunbar, "It involves time investment. If you garner connections with more people, you end up distributing your fixed amount of social capital more thinly so the average capital per person is lower."[25] Because people only have a certain amount of time and energy to put into their friendships, he believes that the result of having a large number of social network friends is that all these friendships become more superficial.

A user's Facebook page shows how many people have sent friend requests and messages, and also indicates other activity. Some users consider Facebook an important part of their social lives.

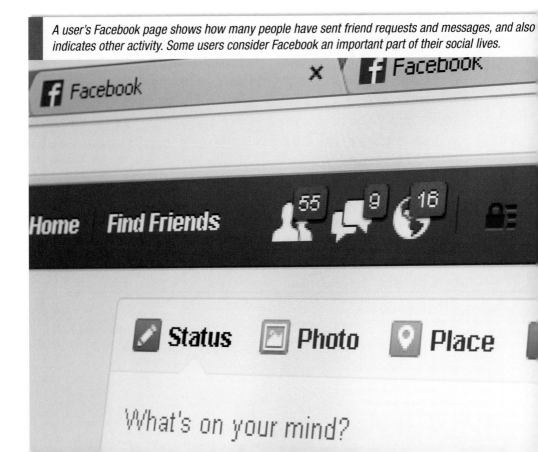

Social Media Is Causing Social Isolation

Sherry Turkle, a psychologist and a professor at the Massachusetts Institute of Technology, argues that as more people rely on social media for connection, there has been a huge decrease in actual conversations between friends, family members, coworkers, and others.

> At home, families sit together, texting and reading e-mail. At work executives text during board meetings. We text (and shop and go on Facebook) during classes and when we're on dates. My students tell me about an important new skill: it involves maintaining eye contact with someone while you text someone else; it's hard, but it can be done. . . . We've become accustomed to a new way of being "alone together." Technology-enabled, we are able to be with one another, and also elsewhere, connected to wherever we want to be. . . . We can end up hiding from one another, even as we are constantly connected to one another.

Sherry Turkle, "The Flight from Conversation," *New York Times*, April 21, 2012. www.nytimes.com.

Others contend that critics should not be so quick to discount the importance of casual friendships or even of social interaction with strangers. Journalist Karol Markowicz argues that the social interaction people have through casual friendships is actually important to psychological well-being. She agrees that it is important to have close friends that a person can rely on in a time of crisis but adds, "For the rest of your life, it's fine to have friends and acquaintances who tell you how cute you look in your profile pictures, play Words with Friends or leave comments when you crowdsource restaurants in a new city."[26] Chief operating officer of Facebook Sheryl Sandberg talks about how important the interaction with strangers was in helping her deal with the death of her husband. She says, "Facebook is helping me get through what has been the hardest year of my life. When I lost my husband suddenly and unexpectedly in May, I felt very isolated—I shared on Facebook and the support of strangers and friends made a huge difference."[27]

Superficial Conversations

In addition to arguing that social media detracts from quality friendships by encouraging too many connections, critics argue that friendships also suffer due to the nature of the social interaction occurring. Members of social media often communicate with many people at once and do so through photos, brief exchanges, or likes. It is also common to browse other people's social media pages without commenting at all. Critics believe this type of interaction is too brief and impersonal and does not help create and maintain strong relationships. Jessi Hempel is a senior writer at *Wired*. She compares the quality of the interactions she has on social media and in person and concludes:

> Daily social media grazing keeps me updated on back-to-school pics and summer vacation destinations, but I don't learn much about how my friends are doing. Last month, I spoke [in person] to a friend who was thinking about leaving a relationship, and another whose father was very ill. Neither conversation was long, but both were revealing. And in talking with my friends, one-on-one, about things that were challenging for them, I felt more connected.[28]

Research shows that many people agree that communicating through social media does not make them feel as deeply connected. For example, research company Euro RSCG Worldwide surveyed 7,213 adults in nineteen countries—including the United States—about their social media use and found a high level of concern over the way that networking is changing the quality of human interaction. The researchers found that more than half of respondents were worried that human-to-human bonds are being weakened by digital communication. They state, "Sure, we may know through social networking what an old friend had for dinner last night and what movie she intends to see this weekend, but we likely haven't had an actual conversation or in-person visit with that friend in some time."[29] The researchers argue that this lack of real conversation means that while many people are learning more about each other than before, they are feeling less connected overall.

> "Daily social media grazing keeps me updated on back-to-school pics and summer vacation destinations, but I don't learn much about how my friends are doing."[28]
>
> —Jessi Hempel is a senior writer at *Wired*.

Creating an Online Persona

Another critique of communication via social media is that many users create and share carefully edited versions of themselves,

A group of young people poses for a selfie during lunch. Many users are selective about things they post on social media so that their friends see them more favorably.

not presenting who they truly are. When a person uses social media, he or she is able to think about and edit comments and images before they are posted. Most users admit that they are selective about what they post so that their friends see them favorably. Law student Thomas White calls this putting up masks and shields, and he argues that as a result of so much editing, many people have a social media presence that is nothing like who they really are. He says, "Have you ever noticed that the lives of your ostensibly boring friends always seem way more interesting on social media sites? That's because these sites and apps allow us to choose an impressive filter for our lives, making boring exceptional and mediocre exciting." He says, "It's a cross between straight up bragging and straight up lying. Social media allow us to put on these masks to become someone we're not."[30] Nineteen-year-old Australian Essena O'Neill had more than eight hundred thousand Instagram followers before she decided to delete her account in 2015. O'Neill explains that while many of her posts appeared spontaneous, they had actually been carefully crafted to create a certain image. She says that there was nothing real about her social media postings, writing, "I made myself into a machine that gave others what they wanted from me, never knowing or valuing my true self."[31]

Investigation reveals that many people feel tremendous pressure to create the perfect online persona. Clinical psychologist Leora Trub talks about how social media never shuts down, and as a result, many people feel like they need to constantly monitor and control their online image. "Before, while you were sleeping, you were sleeping," she says, "Nobody was judging you, and you weren't waking up to an entire other self that existed in this online space that's being commented on."[32] Psychologist and author of *The Big Disconnect* Catherine Steiner-Adair reports that many teens spend hours a day cultivating their online personas. She says, "Girls tell me it's not unusual for them to take two hundred to three hundred photos at one event and then spend two hours agonizing over which three photos to post."[33] In 2014 news websites reported that a nineteen-year-old who lived in England became so consumed with trying to take the perfect selfie that he tried to kill himself.

Social Media's Impact on Emotional Well-Being

It is rare for social media users to be driven to attempt suicide; however, many do report that social media use lowers their self-esteem and leaves them feeling depressed. Some say that they feel unhappy because they think their lives are not as interesting or fun as their friends' lives appear to be. Others say that they feel unhappy after going online and seeing that they were not included in something that their friends were doing. Former reality show star Kim Stolz explains, "Just as quickly as I might scroll through Instagram and see 100 people liked a photo of me, and that makes me feel good, the next moment I might see all of my friends hanging out the night before and wonder why I wasn't invited and feel extremely lonely about that."[34] CNN conducted a study of more than two hundred eighth graders across the United States in order to understand their social networking behavior. The researchers asked study participants about the worst thing that had happened to them on social media. Many of the responses they got were focused on how teens often felt bad after going on social media and seeing what their friends were doing. Responses include:

- Being excluded [from] some parties.
- My best friends hung out without me, and posted it on instagram.
- My friends went out without me and posted pictures on instagram then denied they were out together.
- Not anything specific, but I don't like when people post pictures or tweet about a party that I wasn't invited to.
- Seeing pictures posted by my friends doing things where I wasn't included.[35]

In contrast, other people insist that social networking actually makes people feel happier and more confident. Child clinical psychologist and coauthor of the CNN study Marion K. Underwood notes that while teens did report negative emotions such as feeling excluded, the study also revealed that social media has many positive social effects. She says, "It's a way for them to connect with friends. It's a way for them to see what people are doing. It's a way for them to feel affirmed, supported, lifted up."[36] In a 2015 report, the Pew Research Center found that adults also use social media for social and emotional support. They surveyed 2,003 US adults and found that about 70 percent said they receive support on social media. Pew researchers also investigated social media use by parents specifically and found that two in five parents had received support for parenting issues in the past month, and more than 75 percent said they get useful information from their social networks.

> "[Social media is] a way for [users] to connect with friends. It's a way for them to see what people are doing. It's a way for them to feel affirmed, supported, lifted up."[36]
>
> —Marion K. Underwood is a child clinical psychologist.

Overall, there is mixed evidence on how social media makes users feel. In fact, there is widespread disagreement over the impact that social media has on social interaction in general. What is undeniable is that social interaction has changed as a result of this technology. Researchers and social media users continue to try to understand this change and what it means for the future.

3 Does Social Media Threaten Privacy?

In 2010 Austrian student Max Schrems requested that Facebook send him all the user data it had related to his account. When he received the data CD in the mail, he was shocked to find twelve hundred pages of information detailing everyone he had ever friended or unfriended, all his past messages and postings, locations he logged in from, events he had attended, and more. The record even included things he had deleted. For instance, he says, "I discovered Facebook had kept highly personal messages I had written and then deleted, which, were they to become public, could be highly damaging to my reputation."[37]

Schrems's story highlights the way users of Facebook and other social networks create a digital record that often includes large amounts of personal information. While most people navigating or posting on social media sites are usually focused on communicating with their friends, the Privacy Rights Clearinghouse warns that users also need to remember that anything they do could potentially be viewed or saved by other people—including people they do not know. The advocacy organization says, "As a general rule, before posting something on a social networking profile, imagine it displayed on a billboard on the side of a highway. Would you be uncomfortable to see it there? If so, you may not want to post it at all."[38] Some people dislike the highly public nature of social media and feel that networks threaten their privacy. However, others are not bothered by it. They believe that social media's openness is beneficial to society, and that while it may have caused a change to the type of privacy that people have, this is not harmful.

Control of Personal Information

There is no doubt that the existence of social media has challenged traditional ideas about privacy. Being on social media is very different from socializing in person, because once something is posted online it is easy to lose control over it. When individuals participate in a social network, there is a permanent digital record of what they do, and it is possible that their activities and posts can be viewed and saved by people other than their intended audience and used in ways other than what they intended. Joseph Janes, an associate professor and chair of the Information School of the University of Washington, explains, "Now we lose the ability to differentiate between who gets what. Almost anybody could get almost anything."[39] Even if a person chooses to delete something he or she has posted, it might still exist somewhere online. In a 2014 report, the White House explains that once something is put online, it can be impossible to erase it or control what is done with it. The report reads:

> "As a general rule, before posting something on a social networking profile, imagine it displayed on a billboard on the side of a highway. Would you be uncomfortable to see it there? If so, you may not want to post it at all."[38]
>
> —The Privacy Rights Clearinghouse is a nonprofit organization that works to educate and protect consumers.

In the digital world, information can be captured, copied, shared, and transferred at high fidelity and retained indefinitely. Volumes of data that were once unthinkably expensive to preserve are now easy and affordable to store on a chip the size of a grain of rice. As a consequence, data, once created, is in many cases effectively permanent. Furthermore, digital data often concerns multiple people, making personal control impractical.[40]

Because most people do not have control over how their data is used, critics believe that personal privacy is threatened.

Researchers have found that because people usually do not physically see the audience they are communicating with on social networks, they might be more likely to share personal information that they otherwise would not. Psychiatrist Elias Aboujaoude explains that the feeling of invisibility that comes with being online makes users feel less inhibited. He says, "Being out of sight facilitates problematic actions, not to mention all sorts of outpourings over e-mail, on blogs, in text messages, and in chat rooms."

Aboujaoude explains that psychoanalysts traditionally sat outside their patients' field of vision precisely because having their audience out of sight often encourages people to open up. He says, "Not seeing who we are interacting with increases the chance of a heart-to-heart and of unrestrained effusions of the very personal kind."[41] However, while disinhibition might be helpful in therapy, in the online world it can lead to regrets.

Catherine Steiner-Adair tells a story that illustrates just how quickly and easily an impulsive posting on social media can have unintended and serious effects. She talks about a middle school student who posted a violent, racist, and homophobic comment on a classmate's Facebook page. The boy's parents believed that the boy had heard the ideas elsewhere and had impulsively decided to try them out online. However, the principal decided to expel the student from school. Steiner-Adair points out, "In pre-Facebook days, had this boy spoken this way in the lunchroom or at recess, or even scrawled it as graffiti on the side of the build-

In the same way that a therapist encourages a patient to open up by sitting out of sight, the absence of direct contact often encourages social media users to share content that they might later regret.

ing or in the restroom, his actions would have deserved serious consequences. But the impact of his comments could have been contained."[42] Instead, she says that because these comments were made on social media, he could not take them back, and he had no control over who saw them or how they were shared.

Increased Sharing

Critics argue that not only does the very nature of social networking—which is based on the idea of sharing—threaten privacy, but that the people in control of social networks work hard to erode users' privacy even more by encouraging them to share as much as possible. For example, Christian Fuchs, a professor of social media at the University of Westminster, talks about how Facebook shares user information with advertisers and how users have very little choice about this. He says, "Users must agree to the privacy terms in order to be able to use Facebook and thereby they agree to the use of their self-descriptions, uploaded data and transaction data to be sold to advertising clients. . . . If you do not agree to the privacy terms that make targeted advertising possible, you are unable to use the platform."[43] Critics point out that in addition to social networks forcing users to agree to a certain level of sharing in order to use their services, these sites often encourage sharing in other ways. Social media expert and author of *Sharing Our Lives Online* David R. Brake explains how social networking sites nudge users toward sharing more information about themselves. He says:

> "Not seeing who we are interacting with increases the chance of a heart-to-heart and of unrestrained effusions of the very personal kind."[41]
>
> —Elias Aboujaoude is a psychiatrist.

> Partly this is because of the choices that they offer users—for example, default privacy settings that encourage information sharing and discourage the use of privacy controls where these are offered. Partly also, this is a reflection of what such sites fail to do—for example, they often don't provide their users with a good sense of how many people read what they write or who those people are.[44]

People Publicly Broadcast Too Much Personal Information on Social Media

Arlene Harris writes for the *Irish Examiner*, an online and print newspaper. She argues that rather than communicating with the people who are important to them, many people spend their time on social media trying to share and document every detail of their lives. Harris writes:

> What is it with people nowadays? Everyone seems perpetually compelled to share every detail of their (often mind-numbingly boring) lives with the world. . . . What happened to private moments between loved-ones—surely they are more meaningful than a slushy message on Twitter? And what about memories—isn't it better to watch the concert, firework display, eclipse of the moon or sunrise . . . with your eyes rather than through a lens—so the video of said event can be uploaded as soon as possible? Life is short people, so every moment should be lived for yourself—not for others to validate your existence or even to make them jealous of your amazing lifestyle, body or career—so put down the phone and look around you, there is a whole world out there waiting to be explored.

Arlene Harris, "Do We Share Too Much on Social Media?," *Irish Examiner* (Cork, Ireland), March 29, 2016. www.irishexaminer.com.

However, while many people fear that the pressure to share is threatening their privacy, others contend that privacy is not necessarily about keeping everything hidden. They insist that it is possible for people to share large amounts of personal information on social media and still feel that they have privacy. Writer Nathan Jurgenson explains that while social networking includes a lot of sharing, it also includes concealment of certain information, and this is how users maintain their privacy. He explains, "When you post a photo on Instagram, it offers up not just answers but hints at new questions: Who were you with and why? What were you feeling? What happened between the updates, and why was it left out? Secrets, creative concealments, the spaces between posts—this is where privacy flourishes today."[45] Many social media users agree that while they share many details about their lives online, they also choose to conceal many things, and this is how they maintain privacy.

Concerns About Privacy

Overall, research shows that a significant percentage of people are concerned about how social networking is impacting their privacy. For example, according to a 2016 Pew Research Center report on privacy in the United States, the majority of Americans believe it is very important to control who can get information about them and what information is collected. The Pew researchers report, "They understand that modern life won't allow them to be 'left alone' and untracked, but they do want to have a say in

People Have Become More Selective About the Information They Share on Social Media

In 2016 the social media agency We Are Social published a report about social media trends worldwide. Writer Simon Kemp summarizes their findings, arguing that most people who use social media are no longer focused on broadcasting every detail of their lives to the world but have become more selective about what they share. Kemp states:

> For most people, social is (once again) about conversations: for a few years—namely 2007 to 2014—social media was largely about sharing our lives publicly with the world. That behaviour still exists, but we're becoming more selective about what we share, and whom we share it with. For everyone except marketers, social media is quickly returning to what "social" has always been for human beings: connecting on a personal basis with the people we care about most.

Simon Kemp, "Digital in 2016," We Are Social, January 27, 2016. http://wearesocial.com.

VIEWPOINT

how their personal information is used."[46] However, the researchers found that only 1 percent of those polled said they were very confident that records of their social media activity will stay private and secure. Forty-five percent reported that they were not at all confident that it would. Euro RSCG Worldwide surveyed 7,213 adults in nineteen countries and also found many concerns about privacy. It reports, "A majority of respondents (55 percent) worry that technology is robbing us of our privacy."[47] Researchers found that six out of ten respondents believed that people are wrong to share so many of their personal thoughts and experiences online and that many of those surveyed have had experiences where they regretted doing so. Almost half said that they were worried that friends or family will share something online about them that they do not want to be made public.

Many young people complain that their parents are threatening their privacy by sharing too much about them. It is common for parents to share information and pictures of their children on social media, but research shows that many children are uncomfortable with this. In 2016 researchers Alexis Hiniker, Sarita Y. Schoenebeck, and Julie A. Kientz surveyed 249 parent-child pairs across the United States. They found that children were much more concerned than adults about what was being shared online and were twice as likely to say that adults should not post information about them online without permission. The researchers state, "Child participants reported that they find this content embarrassing and feel frustrated that parents publicly contribute to their online presence without permission."[48] Fourteen-year-old Maisy Hoffman says she dislikes it when her parents make postings about her without permission. She explains:

> I really don't like it when my parents post pictures of me on their social media accounts, especially after finding out that some of my friends follow them. I worry more about my dad. He doesn't always ask if he can post things, so I immediately turn away and ask if he's going to post it. Or I'll find out later because my friend saw something of me on his Instagram and I'll have to ask him to take it down.[49]

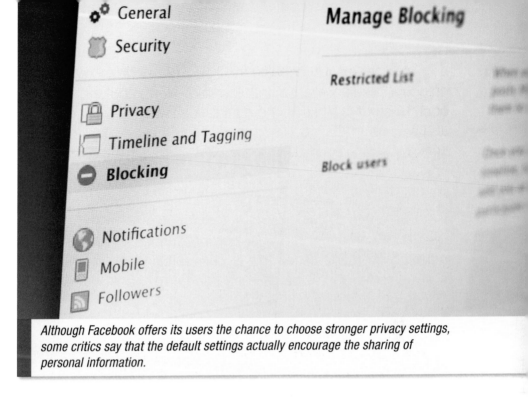

General

Security

Privacy

Timeline and Tagging

Blocking

Notifications

Mobile

Followers

Manage Blocking

Restricted List

Block users

Although Facebook offers its users the chance to choose stronger privacy settings, some critics say that the default settings actually encourage the sharing of personal information.

In addition to young people feeling embarrassed or uncomfortable with what is being shared about them, experts also point out that all these parental postings are contributing to a digital record that these children have no control over.

Yet despite widespread fears that social networking is a threat to privacy, the majority of people continue to use social networks. One of the biggest reasons for this is the belief that social networks are so entrenched in modern life that it is impossible to escape being on them. Social media expert Daniel Trottier explains:

> As use of [social networks] becomes widespread within a given social group, nonparticipation becomes more and more difficult. When network services like Facebook offer a wide variety of functions—not just status updates and picture sharing but messaging and party or event coordination features—those who are not connected can miss out on a variety of social opportunities.[50]

In addition to finding it difficult to socialize without social networking, many people also report that even if they decide not to join a network or make postings, they still end up having an identity on social media because their friends post photos or comments about them.

Information Collection as a Threat to Privacy

Some people believe that the biggest threat to privacy is not the fact that people publicly post personal information online, but the fact that some companies collect information from social media sites and then use it for other purposes, such as advertising or research. In many cases this is completely legal; when people sign up for social media sites and agree to the terms and conditions of those sites, they are usually giving permission for the sites to collect and use their personal data. However, sometimes personal information is used without permission. For example, in 2014 an Oregon woman named Rachele Cateyes posted a photo on her blog of herself in a bikini in order to send a message about having a positive body image. She later discovered that a diet company called Venus Factor was using the photo without her permission as the "before" picture in a "before and after" diet promotion. Whether their data has been taken without permission as Cateyes's was or they have given their permission in order to use the site, many users feel that such a use of their personal information threatens their privacy.

In 2014 Facebook created controversy when it revealed that it had conducted a psychological study on half a million users without their knowledge. As part of a study investigating how emotions are spread on social media, the company manipulated users' news feeds to change the number of negative and positive posts that they saw. Facebook found that people who saw more negative posts were more likely to be negative in their posts and that positive posts were more likely to result in positive postings. Facebook argues that users gave permission for the company to conduct such research when they signed up for Facebook and agreed to the terms of service. However, critics insist that such experimentation without receiving explicit consent is unethical. Jim Sheridan, a member of the Commons media select committee in the United Kingdom, says, "They are manipulating material from people's personal lives and I am worried about the ability of Facebook and others to manipulate people's thoughts in politics or other areas. If people are being thought-controlled in this kind of way there needs to be protection and they at least need to know about it."[51]

While there are many critics of data collection and manipulation by social networks, others believe there is nothing wrong with it and that it can actually be beneficial for consumers. For example, some people like receiving targeted advertising because it shows them products they are interested in. Others enjoy the fact that their postings or photos are being viewed by lots of people. For example, twenty-three-year-old Liza Day Penney from Tennessee says that the clothing company American Eagle Outfitters has used half a dozen of her photos for advertising and even sent her a twenty-five-dollar gift card once. She says she is excited to see her photos online and tries to post photos that the company will use. After she received the gift card, she says, "That was one of the things, too, that really encouraged me to continue to post and continue to tag and hashtag them as I wear the clothes."[52]

> "I am worried about the ability of Facebook and others to manipulate people's thoughts in politics or other areas. If people are being thought-controlled in this kind of way there needs to be protection and they at least need to know about it."[51]
>
> —Jim Sheridan is a member of the Commons media select committee in the United Kingdom.

Monitoring Students' Social Media Accounts

Another controversial subject related to social media and privacy is the way that some schools have begun to monitor students' social media accounts as a way to prevent bullying and violence. It is argued that by identifying threatening behavior on social media, schools can take action to reduce violence. For example, in 2015 Florida's Orange County school district announced that it would start using a program called Snaptrends to monitor students' social media accounts to look for key words such as *gun* or *kill* that might indicate a threat. In defense of its policy, the school board stated: "Because social media can be the source

Teenagers sometimes find that posting something on social media can lead to serious consequences, including bullying at school.

of bullying, school threats or masked cries for help, we believe it is appropriate to monitor public sites where anybody can view comments."[53]

However, others argue that schools should not be allowed to do this. Many students believe that their social media feeds are private conversations that should only be viewed by their friends. "By them monitoring your social media, it's kind of like they're inviting themselves to sit at your kitchen table at Sunday dinner," says student Brooke Lynn Radcliffe. She insists, "It's not okay."[54] Alex Bradshaw works to advance data privacy rights at the Center for Democracy & Technology. He argues that not only is such monitoring an invasion of privacy, but there is no evidence that it is even an effective way to reduce bullying and violence. Further, he argues that it could result in harmful false alarms. He says, "Imagine the occasions when a teen's online joke to their friend that they'd 'die' or 'kill' for something triggers surveillance technology to erroneously report the student to school or local authorities."[55]

As social media becomes an increasingly important part of people's identities and reputations, it is essential to think about privacy. Eric Schmidt and Jared Cohen, who have both worked at Google, argue that in the future people's online identities may become even more important than their offline ones. They insist, "In the future, our identities in everyday life will come to be defined more and more by our virtual activities and associations."[56] This means that people need to be aware of what is happening to their information online, because it could have a significant impact on their lives.

How Does Social Media Affect Politics and World Affairs?

CHAPTER 4

Every four years the United States holds a presidential election, and prior to that election, candidates campaign to get the attention and support of voters. In the 2008 election, Barack Obama became the first candidate to rely heavily on social media for his campaign, using Facebook, Twitter, and Myspace to inform voters and interact with them. Many people believe that his use of social media was a critical part of his victory. Editor in chief of the *Huffington Post* Arianna Huffington, insists, "Were it not for the Internet, Barack Obama would not be president."[57] In addition to helping him win the presidency, it is also widely agreed that Obama's use of social media changed the future of presidential campaigns—and politics in general—by altering the way voters expect politicians to communicate with them. John Allen Hendricks and Dan Schill, editors of the book *Presidential Campaigning and Social Media*, observe that what was novel in 2008 had become essential by the 2012 election. They state, "Obama . . . established a precedent for how future contenders for the White House and political offices below the Oval Office must communicate and interact with the electorate. . . . Politicians must now campaign with Facebook pages, YouTube channels, and Twitter accounts."[58] Elections are not the only place where social media has become essential. In addition to becoming an integral part of the election process, social media has become a major source of information about political and world affairs, as well as an important way for both leaders and regular citizens to communicate about these issues.

An Important Source of News About Current Events

Social media has become a primary source of information for news and commentary on politics and current events. Research shows that a large percentage of people use social media as a source for news. For instance, for the 2015 Reuters Institute Digital News

Report, researchers surveyed more than twenty thousand people in twelve different countries. Forty-one percent of those surveyed said they had used Facebook to find, read, watch, or share news in the previous week. Eighteen percent had used YouTube, and 11 percent had used Twitter. Researchers also found that about a fifth of social media users followed or subscribed to the feed of a political party or politician. Overall, they report that the use of social media for news is growing rapidly. The Media Insight Project studied Americans ages eighteen to thirty-four (often referred to as millennials) and also found that social media is a very important source of news. In a 2015 publication of their findings, the organization says, "Social media plays an enormous role—and for some topics a preeminent one—in how Millennials learn about the world."[59]

> "Politicians must now campaign with Facebook pages, YouTube channels, and Twitter accounts."[58]
>
> —John Allen Hendricks and Dan Schill are editors of the book *Presidential Campaigning and Social Media.*

For instance, twenty-five-year-old Elese explains, "Social media keeps me more informed than I could be with the other forms of news. By quickly scrolling through my feed, I can see the major stories going on. If I need to read deeper into it, I can go to a credible source's website."[60]

While people use hundreds of different social media sites for news about politics and world events, research shows that Facebook dominates. For example, the Pew Research Center reports that about 41 percent of US adults get news on Facebook, while only about 10 percent get it on Twitter. The Media Insight Project finds that 88 percent of Americans ages eighteen to thirty-four get news from Facebook regularly, and that for many of them, the site is one of their most important news sources. It says that of the twenty-four different news and information topics that researchers investigated, Facebook was the main gateway to learning about thirteen of them and the second-most important gateway for seven of the remaining topics.

Giving Individuals a Public Voice

Many people believe that the increasingly powerful role being played by social media in politics and world affairs is beneficial because it allows individual and minority viewpoints to be heard. Before social media, news and information was dispersed to the public by newspapers companies, television networks, and other large entities that had the resources to gather and distribute information. This meant that the governments and companies controlling these media acted as gatekeepers that decided what information was broadcast and what was not. Social media has taken that power away from these groups because it allows any person with an account to potentially reach a very large audience.

In 2008, Barack Obama became the first candidate to use social media to connect with potential voters. Many observers believe that Obama's use of social media was key to his successful campaign.

Some people use that power and freedom to protest social injustices and help mobilize people to change the status quo. For example, activist DeRay Mckesson talks about how social media has helped African Americans tell their story and start a movement against police brutality, a topic on which many believe they have long been silenced. He discusses a 2014 case in which a police officer in Ferguson, Missouri, shot and killed unarmed black teenager Michael Brown. The shooting sparked protests and a movement against police brutality that continues. Social media has played a key role in this movement. Mckesson argues that before social media, African Americans had very little public voice against mistreatment. He says, "The history of blackness is also a history of erasure. Everybody has told the story of black people in struggle except black people. The black people in the struggle haven't had the means to tell the story historically. There were a million slaves but you see very few slave narratives." He explains that social media has changed things by allowing African Americans to be heard in a way they have not been before. He insists, "Missouri would have convinced you that we did not exist if it were not for social media."[61] Instead of being silenced, however, he says that protestors have been able to publicly tell their stories through social media.

The Arab Spring

The power of social media has even been harnessed to help overthrow oppressive governments. The most well-known example is the Arab Spring movement that occurred in the Middle East in 2010 and 2011. Many people in that part of the world were unhappy with the authoritarian and oppressive regimes that governed there; however, nobody had successfully stood up to those regimes. That changed after a Tunisian street vendor set himself on fire to protest the way he had been treated by the government. After that event, large numbers of people began to congregate on social media to talk about what was happening in their country and to make plans to change things. In addition to sharing their stories both within Tunisia and around the world, they used social media to organize massive protests and soon forced the Tunisian

Social media has been used to spread news of important political movements. The Arab Spring movement that occurred in 2010 and 2011 harnessed the power of social media to organize protests in the Middle East.

president and his authoritarian regime to step down. Tunisians then held a democratic election and voted in a new president. In 2011 similar protests led to Egypt's dictator also being pushed out of power. The success of these events inspired protests in a number of other Middle Eastern countries, including Libya and Syria.

Many people insist that none of these events would have been possible without social media. They argue that oppressive governments kept the population under their control by making them afraid to speak up. Mohammad-Munir Adi, author of *The Usage of Social Media in the Arab Spring*, insists, "Fear is one constant that held the people back from revolting against their oppressors on such a large scale years before."[62] However, it is argued that social media allowed people to overcome their fear by understanding they were not alone and that by joining together as a group they had the power to make a change. Journalist Saleem Kassim explains, "Social networks have broken the psychological barrier

46

of fear by helping many to connect and share information. It has given most people in the Arab world the knowledge that they are not alone, that there are others experiencing just as much brutality, just as much hardships, just as much lack of justice."[63]

However, while many people are enthusiastic about the power of social networks to help fight oppression and cause change, skeptics contend that not everything broadcast on social media is beneficial to society. They point out that because anybody can use social media to make a statement or spread a message, it can just as easily be used to spread misinformation or to facilitate oppression as it can to fight these things. For example, oppressive leaders and governments can easily use social media to spread their own messages, or they can even shut it down altogether. Some people argue that the Arab Spring movement was only successful because at that time using social media for social change was a relatively new concept, and governments did not understand what protestors were doing. Journalist Jessi Hempel argues that the liberating effect of social media in the Middle East did not last long, because governments quickly learned to shut it down in order to stop activists and even started using it themselves to spread misinformation. In addition, she says that militant groups are using social media for their own causes, further contributing to instability and violence in that part of the world. In fact, she says, "As it turns out, bad people are also very good at social media." Overall, she believes that social media actually changed very little, observing in 2016, "Half a decade later, the Middle East is roiling in violence and repression."[64]

> "As it turns out, bad people are also very good at social media."[64]
>
> —Jessi Hempel is a journalist.

Social Media and Diversity of Ideas

While social media is clearly a powerful way of spreading information and ideas—whether for good or bad—there is disagreement about the types of information and ideas social media exposes people to. Advocates praise social media sites as forums that encourage free expression and the exposure to alternative points of view, insisting that they help broaden people's views. However,

Social Media Facilitates Freedom of Expression

Pierre Omidyar is the founder and chair of eBay and CEO of First Look Media. He insists that social media gives people the ability to freely express themselves like never before. Omidyar explains:

> I believe that social media is a tool of liberation and empowerment. That may seem fairly audacious when a good portion of the Western world is using Facebook and Twitter to post pictures of what they had for dinner or take quizzes on what TV character they may be. But the freedom to communicate openly and honestly is not something to be taken for granted. In countries where traditional media is a tool of control, these new and truly social channels have the power to radically alter our world. In my eyes, social media is one of the most important global leaps forward in recent human history. It provides for self-expression and promotes mutual understanding.

Pierre Omidyar, "Social Media: Enemy of the State or Power to the People?," *Huffington Post*, February 27, 2014. www.huffingtonpost.com.

---

critics contend that while this is theoretically possible, in reality most people are only exposed to a narrow range of ideas on social media. Economist Brian Knight explains that unlike traditional news sources, social media is personalized according to users' friendships and interests. He explains, "Two users of Twitter might be exposed to very different content based on which accounts they choose to follow, while two people reading the local newspaper might read different stories but at the end of the day it's the same content they're exposed to."[65] Exactly what individuals encounter on social media is determined by a number of different factors, including their friends and the people they follow, their likes and interests, and the way their feeds are organized by social media sites. Critics worry that because social media feeds are usually personalized to show people things that they like or are interested in, they will not be exposed to alternative points of view. Further, researchers have found that people who get their news on social media often stumble across it rather than actively looking for it, meaning that they are unlikely to seek out anything that does not appear in their news feeds or home pages.

On the other hand, some observers contend that social media exposes users to a variety of sources, and further, they insist that users do not just passively read what pops up in front of them but take a much more active role in seeking news and information on social media. For example, Media Insight Project researchers found that millennials are actually drawn to news they might have

Social Media Does Not Facilitate Freedom of Expression

Researchers from the Pew Research Center explain the results of a study that shows social media does not encourage people to freely express their opinions:

[There is a] tendency of people not to speak up about policy issues in public . . . when they believe their own point of view is not widely shared. This tendency is called the "spiral of silence." Some social media creators and supporters have hoped that social media platforms like Facebook and Twitter might produce different enough discussion venues that those with minority views might feel freer to express their opinions, thus broadening public discourse and adding new perspectives to everyday discussion of political issues. We set out to study this by conducting a survey of 1,801 adults. It focused on one important public issue: Edward Snowden's 2013 revelations of widespread government surveillance of Americans' phone and email records. . . . Overall, the findings indicate that in the Snowden case, social media did not provide new forums for those who might otherwise remain silent to express their opinions and debate issues.

Keith Hampton et al., "Social Media and the 'Spiral of Silence,'" Pew Research Center, August 26, 2014. www.pewinternet.org.

VIEWPOINT

otherwise ignored because their friends are recommending it and contextualizing it. They also found that users actively make choices about the sources that appear in their feeds and whether these sources are reliable. The researchers state, "Once they encounter news . . . nearly 9 in 10 report usually seeing diverse opinions, and three-quarters of those report investigating opinions different than their own."[66] In the 2015 Reuters Institute Digital News Report, researchers also concluded that social media helps users find more diverse forms of news.

Social Media and Leadership

In addition to disagreement over how social media influences the content of the news and information people get, there is also disagreement over how it influences the actions of politicians and other leaders. Social media makes it much easier for citizens to access information about the government and politicians. As a result, some argue that it promotes transparency and accountability by holding leaders more accountable for what they do. David Chavern, president and CEO of the Newspaper Association of America, argues that transparency is essential in a good government. "Transparency in government is essential to upholding American democracy," he writes. "When citizens have access to behind-the-scenes information about local and federal administrations, politicians are held accountable. The public is educated and engaged."[67] He believes that overall, transparency makes the US system of government stronger.

"Too many politicians aren't voting their conscience, they're voting to placate blog commenters, and that's no way to run government."[68]

—Wesley Donehue is a political strategist.

However, critics charge that sometimes the transparency and accountability of social media actually has a negative effect. Because of social media, many political figures have the public following and commenting on everything they do. Political strategist Wesley Donehue argues that when there is so much public scrutiny, politicians may start focusing on trying to keep a good image on social media, rather than on doing their jobs properly. He gives an example of how this

Many political figures, such as Donald Trump, make extensive use of social media and can have millions of followers. Some critics say the use of social media causes public officials to focus too much on their image, rather than important issues.

can be harmful. He says that politicians need the freedom to keep an open mind and consider a wide range of ideas, including ideas that are unpopular with voters. In his opinion, this is part of the process of making good decisions. Donehue explains, "In policy making, lots of ideas are thrown out in order to set the good apart from the bad, and in order to stake out a position for compromise." However, because of social media, says Donehue, if a politician even mentions an unpopular idea, he or she is likely to be subject to widespread public criticism. As a result, he says, "Too many politicians aren't voting their conscience, they're voting to placate blog commenters, and that's no way to run government."[68]

Critics also worry that the prominence of social media forces politicians to continually perform for the public, rather than focusing on their jobs. Freelance writer Sheryl Kraft explains that in order to be successful on social media, a person must continually give his or her readers new and interesting information or risk being quickly overshadowed by someone else more exciting. She says, "You have to have something to say—preferably dramatic—almost all the time. Because if you don't, your readers will lose interest and forget you ever existed."[69] Journalist and author Nicholas Carr agrees. He says that social media forces politicians to constantly work to keep their followers. He states, "Authority and respect don't accumulate on social media; they have to be earned anew at each moment. You're only as relevant as your last tweet."[70] Some people worry that when politicians focus on constantly making new and interesting social media posts, they do not perform their jobs as well.

> "The internet empowers each one of us to speak, create, learn and share."[71]
>
> —Vinton Cerf is vice president of Google.

A New Freedom

Despite critiques such as this, there is widespread enthusiasm about the use of social media in politics and world affairs. Vinton Cerf, vice president of Google, points out that social media allows a freedom of expression and access to information that many people have never had before. He says, "The internet empowers each one of us to speak, create, learn and share."[71] Many people agree, and social media continues to play an increasingly prominent role in current events around the world.

5 Are People Too Dependent on Social Media?

Writer and editor Larry Carlat says that he started using Twitter simply as a way to make a few friends laugh. However, he explains that he quickly became consumed with the social media site and was soon posting twenty to thirty times a day, every day of the week. "Soon my entire life revolved around tweeting," he recalled. "I stopped reading, rarely listened to music or watched TV. When I was out with friends, I would duck into the bathroom with my iPhone. I tweeted while driving, between sets of tennis, even at the movies." Carlat says that even when he was not using Twitter, it was never far from his thoughts. He explains, "When I wasn't on Twitter, I would compose faux aphorisms [fake but witty sayings] that I might use later. I began to talk that way too. . . . I posted every hour on the hour, day and night, using a Web site that enabled me to tweet while asleep. It was an obsession."[72] After losing his job, Carlat realized that Twitter had taken over his life, and he finally decided to quit. While his story is extreme, his compulsion to use social media is not unusual. It is easy to find stories from people who say they feel a strong attachment to social media sites like Twitter and feel compelled to use them often. There is disagreement over the implications of this. Some observers believe that many people depend too much on social media and that this has negative consequences. Others contend that social media sites have become an important part of modern life and that it is normal and healthy to use them often.

Social Media Addiction

According to some researchers, dependence on social media is an unhealthy addiction. There is evidence that social media use does cause chemical reactions in the body that mirror the types of responses noted in other forms of addiction. These researchers believe that social media use causes the brain to release a neurotransmitter called dopamine, which is a physiological reward that produces a pleasurable feeling. Therefore, one reason people might spend a lot of time using social media is because they want to keep feeling the pleasure associated with dopamine release. Former reality show star Kim Stolz explains that it is the constant stream of feedback and new information from social media that stimulates the brain to release dopamine. She says, "I think when you see your phone light up from across the room, it's that ping of dopamine in your system. You get that euphoric, excited feeling, and I think that's addictive. Now we text people, we Instagram, we Vine, we Tinder just to feel that again. And the more we do it, the more we get it back, so it becomes a very addictive process."[73] As with drug use, the pleasurable feeling tapers over time. Tony Schwartz, author of *The Way We're Working Isn't Working*, explains that just as a drug addict builds up a tolerance and requires more and more of a drug to feel the same high, over time social media users need more and more stimulation in order to keep feeling pleasure. He says, "The brain's craving for novelty, constant stimulation and immediate gratification creates something called a 'compulsion loop.' Like lab rats and drug addicts, we need more and more to get the same effect."[74]

Stories from social media users reveal that it is common to feel physically addicted to using that media. For example, a 2016 *Huffington Post* article includes confessions from Whisper, an app that lets people make anonymous confessions. One user confesses, "I'm so addicted to social media and the internet I don't really sleep anymore."[75] And another says, "I'm so addicted to social media that I that I can't even put my phone down in the shower."[76] In 2015 the journal *Social Media + Society* published a paper by researchers from Cornell University's information science program. The researchers studied people who pledged to stop using Facebook for ninety-nine days. They found that many who withdrew from the social media site and had a lot of trouble staying off it. For example, one person said, "In the first 10 days, I thought about Facebook a lot. Whenever I opened up a browser, my fingers would automatically go to 'f'. On day 9, I had a dream about accidentally logging in to Facebook."[77] Another described the experience: "Like I was going through withdrawal from an addiction! I had to resist the urge to check it every few minutes."[78] And still another reported that

The Facebook app notifies a user of new activity on their account. Many users say that they become addicted to using social media, often feeling that they are missing out by refraining from constantly logging into their accounts.

the compulsion was so strong that it was impossible to resist, stating, "I caved in after about a week, and began checking FB a few times a day for about a week. But then I decided to quit FB again, which again only last 2-3 days. For the past 4 days I have been checking FB once-twice a day, spending around 5 min per day in total."[79] Overall, the researchers found that while many of the study participants pledged to stay off Facebook for ninety-nine days, many were unable to do so.

Addicting by Design

Not only can the constant feedback and new information from social media make users feel as if they are missing out if they refrain from logging in, but designers actually work very hard to make their social media sites as addicting as possible. Blogger Nir Eyal explains, "Since these services rely on advertising revenue, the more frequently you use them, the more money they make. It's no wonder these companies employ teams of people focused on engineering their services to be as engaging as possible. These products aren't habit-forming by chance; it's by design. They have an incentive to keep us hooked."[80] Tristan Harris, a design ethicist who is also a product philosopher at Google, talks about just how hard it is to resist all the efforts that go into make these sites addicting. He says, "The 'I don't have enough willpower' conversation misses the fact that there are 1,000 people on the other side of the screen whose job is to break down the self-regulation that you have."[81]

> "Since these services rely on advertising revenue, the more frequently you use them, the more money they make. . . . These products aren't habit-forming by chance; it's by design. They have an incentive to keep us hooked."[80]
>
> —Nir Eyal is a blogger.

Some people feel like they have become so dependent on social media that they seek professional treatment for that dependency. In the United States there are a number of facilities and programs for addiction to social media and other Internet activities. For example, reSTART is an addiction rehab center in Washington State, where addicts stay for eight to twelve weeks and learn how to use digital technology without it taking over their lives. At Outback Therapeutic Expeditions in Utah, teens counter addiction by taking part in various wilderness activities, including hiking and learning how to build fires and construct shelters. Camp Grounded is technology-free summer camp designed for adults.

A Natural Desire to Be Connected

While some people find themselves at facilities like reSTART because social media has become all-consuming, critics insist that for most people, dependency on social media is not a true medical addiction on par with, say, chemical dependency. Instead, these commentators argue that the majority of people depend on social media simply because it has become such an integral part of life, and this dependence is not harmful. Bradford Health Services, which provides treatment for numerous types of addiction, points out that simply using social media a lot or saying that you cannot live without it does not necessarily mean addiction. The treatment center explains, "We now live in a technological age. For example, most of us would struggle with maintaining a household if we could not use any appliances for 24 hours. Does that mean we are addicted to appliances? No, of course not. Not being able to function when a wide array of things we use every day are no longer available to us is pretty normal."[82]

Senior writer at *Wired* Jessi Hempel says that in 2015 she did her third annual monthlong social media cleanse by resolving not to use social media sites for a month. However, she says that she cheated several times. Her explanation reveals how social media has become an important part of everyday life:

> Some of the cheats were purposeful. Once I needed an address for an event I planned to attend, and the invitation was on Facebook. Another time, I was getting ready to interview a story subject, and I wanted some background on her before we spoke. Most of the time, though, my slips were accidental. I discovered (again this year) that social software is embedded everywhere. My Facebook log-in doubled as my log-in for my ride-sharing app (Uber), my jogging music app (RockMyRun), my house-sharing app (Airbnb), and my bike-riding app (MapMyRide). And then there was Rise, the social app I use to send photos of my meals to a professional dietician, who advises me to leave off the chocolate and add a bit of spinach. Wasn't that basically a social app? Then I traveled to a country that had expensive data, and I didn't want to pay for a plan. I decided to use Wi-Fi to call home, and turned to Google Hangouts to video chat, send photos and generally keep in touch. It was all over. Social media won.[83]

As Hempel's story reveals, some people use social media all the time, not because they feel physically addicted to being on it, but simply because it makes their lives easier.

Social Media as a Distraction

In addition to worrying about addiction, some critics fear that heavily depending on social media is harmful because it distracts from other important activities such as work or homework. For

Some critics say that using social media distracts teenage users from important activities. One study found that 50 percent of teens used social media while doing their homework.

example, researchers have found that a significant percentage of young people connect over social media while doing homework and that this reduces the quality of their homework. Common Sense Media found that about 50 percent of teens typically use social media while they do homework, with only a small number of them saying that this use was related to their assignment. Fifty-five percent of them did not believe that their social media use had a negative impact on the quality of their work. However, some experts insist that this is not the case, because the brain is physically unable to do both tasks well at the same time. University of Michigan psychology professor David Meyer explains:

> Under most conditions, the brain simply cannot do two complex tasks at the same time. It can happen only when the two tasks are both very simple and when they don't compete with each other for the same mental resources. An example would be folding laundry and listening to the weather report on the radio. That's fine. But listening to a lecture while texting, or doing homework and being on Facebook—each of these tasks is very demanding, and each of them uses the same area of the brain, the prefrontal cortex.[84]

As a result, Meyer and others claim that when a person tries to use social media and do something like homework at the same time, the quality of that other task suffers.

Others contend that social media is actually a useful tool that can be successfully integrated into work and homework. For example, students can use social media to discuss assignments, get answers to questions, and engage in group study sessions. Some people insist that social media is so valuable that teachers should actually make more of an effort to integrate it into homework time. Educational technology professor at Rowan University Shawna Bu Shell maintains that if social media was better integrated into the classroom, students would be less likely to use it in distracting ways. "My research shows students are not distracted if homework is designed well," she insists. "If a teacher is good at designing

> "Under most conditions, the brain simply cannot do two complex tasks at the same time. It can happen only when the two tasks are both very simple and when they don't compete with each other for the same mental resources."[84]
>
> —David Meyer is a psychology professor at the University of Michigan.

Teens Are Too Dependent on Their Cell Phones

TeenSafe is a service that allows parents to monitor their children's phone use, including social media activity. On its website, the organization insists that many teens become addicted to using their cell phones for social networking and other activities:

> We often joke our children are inseparable from their cell phones, but smartphone addiction has become a serious issue facing our teens. . . . Everyday we witness our sons and daughters FaceTiming, Snapchatting, or sharing Instagrams during random moments with their friends. We all know how smartphones and social media has changed the way our teens communicate, but recent evidence shows that smartphone addiction can affect our teen's health in ways we never imagined.

TeenSafe, "How Does Smartphone Addiction Affect Teen Health?," June 16, 2015. www.teensafe.com.

homework and is willing to integrate social media, then students won't be sneaking, trying to use it."[85]

Dependency as a Cause of Stress

Another worry about social media dependency is that constant connection causes people to feel stressed because they worry that they might miss out on something. In 2015 the Australian Psychological Society released its annual survey about stress and well-being in Australia. Researchers found that many people—particularly teens—feel pressured to maintain constant connection for fear of missing out. For example, 79 percent of teen respondents said, "I am afraid that I will miss something if I don't stay connected to my online social networks," and 42 percent said, "I get anxious when I don't know what my friends are up to."[86] Overall, approximately one in ten of those surveyed—both adults and teens—said that keeping up with social media is a cause of stress in their lives. Australian teen Allaina Dargel explains, "Because

I use social media to communicate with my friends and family, when I am unable to access these sites I am paranoid and afraid that I have missed something they have said."[87] She says that checking Facebook is the first thing she does when she wakes up and is frequently the last thing she does before she goes to bed.

Although some people do report that their constant connection to social media is stressful, others insist that this is not the case. The Pew Research Center surveyed 1,801 US adults and found that while it is often assumed that people who spend a lot of time on social media have higher levels of stress, this is actually not true. It found that some people do feel more stress as a result of being informed about stressful events in their friends'

Constant Cell Phone Connection Is Not Harmful for Teens

Psychology professor Ira Hyman argues that there is nothing wrong with teens constantly using their phones for social networking and other types of communication. Hyman explains:

> Feeling a need to be socially connected hardly seems like an addiction to me. . . . Staying constantly in touch with your entire circle of friends may be the new norm in tech-land. Although I find it odd to interrupt a live conversation to respond to a text message, I didn't grow up in tech-land. I'm not a native. The natives of tech-land, these wonderful young adults, are developing their own rules for social interaction. To an outsider, they may appear addicted to their cell phones. But I see an emerging form of social interaction in tech-land. These young adults are defining what forms of cell phone use are normal. And if being constantly in touch through your cell phone is normal, then it probably isn't an addiction.

Ira Hyman, "Are You Addicted to Your Cellphone?," *Psychology Today*, March 27, 2013. www .psychologytoday.com.

VIEWPOINT

Experts say that a significant number of social media users suffer stress from being worried that they are missing out on something their friends are doing online.

lives. However, the organization reports that overall, there is no evidence of people feeling stressed about keeping up or missing out. It says that in general, social media users are not more likely to feel stress than nonusers. In fact, Pew researchers found that many women who use social media actually have lower levels of stress. They report, "Compared with a woman who does not use these technologies, a women who uses Twitter several times per day, sends or receives 25 emails per day, and shares two digital pictures through her mobile phone per day, scores 21% lower on our stress measure than a woman who does not use these technologies at all."[88] The researchers suggest that the lower stress level may be because the act of sharing through social media actually reduces stress levels.

A Plugged-In World

Whether or not people are too dependent on social media, and whether or not this is harmful, the fact is that social media has become so entrenched in modern society that it seems impossible to escape a certain level of dependency. Journalist Kristen V. Brown visited the reSTART addiction treatment center in Washington State and found that unplugging from social media and other digital media did seem to make many people happier. She says, "Everybody at reSTART enthuses about how peaceful they feel now that they've unplugged. It was hard not to feel like the reSTART lifestyle was one in which we all might be a little better off." Yet she argues that online activities have become such an integral part of life that unplugging seems unrealistic, even if it does have some benefits. She says, "Can these addicts maintain that calm once re-immersed in the plugged-in world? Can any of us? The addiction to technology is a societal one. Breaking it would require a cultural commitment to rethinking the way we live today."[89] Based on the way that social media extends its reach every day, such a cultural change seems unlikely. Instead, for better or worse, social media has become a part of life for most people.

> "The addiction to technology is a societal one. Breaking it would require a cultural commitment to rethinking the way we live today."[89]
>
> —Kristen V. Brown is a journalist.

SOURCE NOTES

Introduction: An Essential Part of Life

1. Quoted in Colin Daileda, "Obama to Astronaut Scott Kelly: 'Make Sure to Instagram' When up in Space," *Mashable*, January 20, 2015. www.mashable.com.
2. Heather Ciras, "How Scott Kelly Became a Social Media Superstar—in Space," *Boston Globe*, March 3, 2016. www.bostonglobe.com.
3. Gallup, "The Myth of Social Media," *Wall Street Journal*, 2014. http://online.wsj.com.
4. Maeve Duggan et al., "Parents and Social Media: Mothers Are Especially Likely to Give and Receive Support on Social Media," Pew Research Center, July 16, 2015. www.pewinternet.org.
5. James P. Steyer, *Talking Back to Facebook: The Common Sense Guide to Raising Kids in the Digital Age*. New York: Scribner, 2012, p. 7.
6. Quoted in Alan Greenblatt, "Not-So-Social Media: Why People Have Stopped Talking on Phones," NPR, May 9, 2014. www.npr.org.
7. Steyer, *Talking Back to Facebook*, p. 8.

Chapter 1: What Are the Facts?

8. Simon Kemp, "Digital in 2016," We Are Social, January 27, 2016. http://wearesocial.com.
9. Kemp, "Digital in 2016."
10. Lulu Chang, "Americans Spend an Alarming Amount of Time Checking Social Media on Their Phones," Digital Trends, June 13, 2015. www.digitaltrends.com.
11. Common Sense Media, "The Common Sense Census: Media Use by Tweens and Teens," 2015. www.commonsensemedia.org.
12. Marion K. Underwood and Robert W. Faris, "Being 13: Perils of Lurking on Social Media," CNN, October 6, 2015. www.cnn.com.
13. Common Sense Media, "The Common Sense Census."

14. Mark Fidelman, "The New Social Media Trend That Will Dominate Political Elections in 2016," *Forbes*, February 12, 2016. www.forbes.com.

15. Federal Bureau of Investigation, "Cyber Tip: Social Media and the Use of Personal Information," *News Blog*, October 27, 2015. www.fbi.gov.

16. Quoted in Mary Catherine Wellons, "11 Predictions on the Future of Social Media," CNBC, 2014. www.cnbc.com.

Chapter 2: How Does Social Media Affect Social Interaction?

17. Sophie Laing, "This Gen-Z Teenager Explains Why and How She Uses Various Social Media Platforms," Social Media Week, June 24, 2015. http://socialmediaweek.org.

18. Quoted in Kim Garst, "How Social Media Impacts People's Lives Every Day (for the Good!)," *Boom Social*, February 11, 2014. http://kimgarst.com.

19. Drew Hendricks, "Are Interest-Based Networks the Way of the Future?," *Forbes*, October 16, 2014. www.forbes.com.

20. Joani, comment on Otis Chandler, "50 Million Reviews!," Goodreads, April 6, 2016. www.goodreads.com.

21. Lu, comment on Chandler, "50 Million Reviews!"

22. Dennis Merritt Jones, "The Spiritual Side of Facebook," *Huffington Post*, January 13, 2012. www.huffingtonpost.com.

23. danah boyd, *It's Complicated: The Social Lives of Networked Teens*. New Haven, CT: Yale University Press, 2014, pp. 20–21.

24. Quoted in Drake Bennett, "The Dunbar Number, from the Guru of Social Networks," Bloomberg, January 11, 2013. www.bloomberg.com.

25. Quoted in Maria Konnikova, "The Limits of Friendship," *New Yorker*, October 7, 2014. www.newyorker.com.

26. Karol Markowicz, "Yes, Social Media Friendships Are Real," *New York Post*, February 7, 2016. http://nypost.com.

27. Quoted in Quora, "Session with Sheryl Sandberg," December 15, 2015. http://quora.com.

28. Jessi Hempel, "Why I Quit My Facebook Quitting," *Wired*, September 20, 2015. www.wired.com.

29. Euro RSCG Worldwide, "Prosumer Report: This Digital Life," 2012. www.havasww.de.

30. Thomas White, "Why Social Media Isn't Social," *Huffington Post*, September 4, 2013. www.huffingtonpost.com.

31. Quoted in Valeriya Safronova, "On Fake Instagram, a Chance to Be Real," *New York Times*, November 18, 2015. www.nytimes.com.

32. Quoted in Safronova, "On Fake Instagram, a Chance to Be Real."

33. Catherine Steiner-Adair with Teresa H. Barker, *The Big Disconnect: Protecting Childhood and Family Relationships in the Digital Age*. New York: HarperCollins, 2013, p. 208.

34. Quoted in Eliana Dockterman, "Kim Stolz: How Social Media Is Ruining Our Relationships," *Time*, June 24, 2014. http://time.com.

35. Underwood and Faris, "Being 13."

36. Quoted in Chuck Hadad, "Why Some 13-Year-Olds Check Social Media 100 Times a Day," CNN, October 13, 2015. www.cnn.com.

Chapter 3: Does Social Media Threaten Privacy?

37. Quoted in Helen Pidd, "Facebook Could Face €100,000 Fine for Holding Data That Users Have Deleted," *Guardian* (Manchester), October 20, 2011. www.theguardian.com.

38. Privacy Rights Clearinghouse, "Fact Sheet 35: Social Networking Privacy: How to Be Safe, Secure and Social," February 2016. www.privacyrights.org.

39. Joseph Janes, "None of Your Beeswax: Privacy Matters, but Why?," *American Libraries*, May 2014. http://americanlibrariesmagazine.org.

40. White House, "Big Data: Seizing Opportunities, Preserving Values," May 2014. www.whitehouse.gov.

41. Elias Aboujaoude, *Virtually You: The Dangerous Powers of the E-personality*, New York: Norton, 2011, p. 41.

42. Steiner-Adair with Barker, *The Big Disconnect*, p. 47.

43. Christian Fuchs, *Social Media: A Critical Introduction*. Los Angeles: Sage, 2014, pp. 166–67.

44. David R. Brake, *Sharing Our Lives Online: Risks and Exposure in Social Media*. New York: Palgrave Macmillan, 2014, p. 10.

45. Nathan Jurgenson, "Hiding in Public," *Wired*, April 2014. http://wiredmag.com.

46. Lee Rainie, "The State of Privacy in America: What We Learned," Pew Research Center, January 20, 2016. www.pewresearch.org.

47. Euro RSCG Worldwide, "Prosumer Report."

48. Alexis Hiniker, Sarita Y. Schoenebeck, and Julie A. Kientz, "Not at the Dinner Table: Parents' and Children's Perspectives on Family Technology Rules," paper presented at the Association for Computing Machinery's Conference on Computer-Supported Cooperative Work and Social Computing in San Francisco, March 2, 2016. http://media.wix.com.

49. Quoted in KJ Dell'Antonia, "Don't Post About Me on Social Media, Children Say," *Well* (blog), *New York Times*, March 8, 2016. http://well.blogs.nytimes.com.

50. Daniel Trottier, *Identity Problems in the Facebook Era*. New York: Routledge, 2014, p. 143.

51. Quoted in Robert Booth, "Facebook Reveals News Feed Experiment to Control Emotions," *Guardian* (Manchester), June 29, 2014. www.theguardian.com.

52. Quoted in Sydney Ember and Rachel Abrams, "On Instagram and Other Social Media, Redefining 'User Engagement,'" *New York Times*, September 20, 2015. www.nytimes.com.

53. Quoted in Eun Kyung Kim, "Safety or Snooping? Schools Start Monitoring Social Media Accounts of Students," *Today*, September 3, 2015. www.today.com.

54. Quoted in Kim, "Safety or Snooping? Schools Start Monitoring Social Media Accounts of Students."

55. Alex Bradshaw, "States Take Steps to Limit School Surveillance of Student Social Media Pages," Center for Democracy & Technology, January 27, 2016. https://cdt.org.

56. Eric Schmidt and Jared Cohen, *The New Digital Age: Reshaping the Future of People, Nations and Business*. New York: Knopf, 2013, p. 32.

Chapter 4: How Does Social Media Affect Politics and World Affairs?

57. Quoted in Claire Cain Miller, "How Obama's Internet Campaign Changed Politics," *Bits* (blog), *New York Times*, November 7, 2008. http://bits.blogs.nytimes.com.

58. John Allen Hendricks and Dan Schill, eds., *Presidential Campaigning and Social Media: An Analysis of the 2012 Campaign*. New York: Oxford University Press, 2015, p. xxi.

59. American Press Institute, "How Millennials Get News: Inside the Habits of America's First Digital Generation," March 16, 2015. www.americanpressinstitute.org.

60. Quoted in American Press Institute, "How Millennials Get News."

61. Quoted in Noah Berlatsky, "Hashtag Activism Isn't a Cop-Out," *Atlantic*, January 7, 2015. www.theatlantic.com.

62. Mohammad-Munir Adi, *The Usage of Social Media in the Arab Spring: The Potential of Media to Change Political Landscapes Throughout the Middle East and Africa*. Zurich: LIT Verlag, 2014, p. 16.

63. Saleem Kassim, "Twitter Revolution: How the Arab Spring Was Helped by Social Media," PolicyMic, July 3, 2013. http://mic.com.

64. Jessi Hempel, "Social Media Made the Arab Spring, but Couldn't Save It," *Wired*, January 26, 2016. www.wired.com.

65. Quoted in Claire Cain Miller, "Social Media Deepens Partisan Divides. But Not Always," *New York Times*, November 20, 2014. www.nytimes.com.

66. American Press Institute, "How Millennials Get News."

67. David Chavern, "Sunshine Week: Encouraging Increased Transparency in Government in 2016," Newspaper Association of America, March 2016. www.naa.org.

68. Wesley Donehue, "The Danger of Twitter, Facebook Politics," CNN, April 24, 2012. www.cnn.com.

69. Sheryl Kraft, "Why I'll Never Win a Blogging Award," *Huffington Post*, March 7, 2014. www.huffingtonpost.com.

70. Nicholas Carr, "How Social Media Is Ruining Politics," *Politico*, September 2, 2015. www.politico.com.

71. Vinton Cerf, "'Father of the Internet': Why We Must Fight for Its Freedom," CNN, November 30, 2012. http://edition.cnn.com.

Chapter 5: Are People Too Dependent on Social Media?

72. Larry Carlat, "Confessions of a Tweeter," *New York Times Magazine*, November 11, 2011. www.nytimes.com.

73. Quoted in Dockterman, "Kim Stolz."

74. Tony Schwartz, "Addicted to Distraction," *New York Times*, November 28, 2015. www.nytimes.com.

75. Quoted in Kate Bratskeir, "21 Confessions from People Who Are Addicted to Social Media," *Huffington Post*, January 29, 2016. www.huffingtonpost.com.

76. Quoted in Bratskeir, "21 Confessions from People Who Are Addicted to Social Media."

77. Quoted in Eric P.S. Baumer et al., "Missing Photos, Suffering Withdrawal, or Finding Freedom? How Experiences of Social Media Non-use Influence the Likelihood of Reversion," *Social Media + Society*, July–December 2015. http://sms.sagepub.com.

78. Quoted in Baumer et al., "Missing Photos, Suffering Withdrawal, or Finding Freedom? How Experiences of Social Media Non-use Influence the Likelihood of Reversion."

79. Quoted in Baumer et al., "Missing Photos, Suffering Withdrawal, or Finding Freedom? How Experiences of Social Media Non-use Influence the Likelihood of Reversion."

80. Nir Eyal, "Who's Really Addicting Us to Technology?," *Huffington Post*, February 5, 2016. www.huffingtonpost.com.

81. Quoted in Natasha Singer, "Can't Put Down Your Device? That's by Design," *New York Times*, December 5, 2015. www.nytimes.com.

82. Bradford Health Services, "Social Media Addiction: Genuine Disorder or Joke?," 2016. http://bradfordhealth.com.

83. Hempel, "Why I Quit My Facebook Quitting."

84. Quoted in *The Brilliant Blog*, "The Problem with Media Multitasking While Reading," Annie Murphy Paul, May 3, 2013. http://anniemurphypaul.com.

85. Quoted in Phil Dunn, "Students Say Social Media Interfere with Homework," *USA Today*, January 15, 2013. www.usatoday.com.

86. Australian Psychological Society, "Stress & Wellbeing: How Australians Are Coping with Life," November 2015. www.psychology.org.au.

87. Quoted in Michelle Gately, "Aussie Teens Feel Stressed After Constant Social Media," *Bulletin* (Sydney), November 12, 2015. www.themorningbulletin.com.au.

88. Keith Hampton et al., "Social Media and the Cost of Caring," Pew Research Center, January 15, 2015. www.pewinternet.org.

89. Kristen V. Brown, "These People Are So Addicted to the Internet That They Had to Go to Rehab," *Fusion*, August 10, 2015. http://fusion.net.

Center for Safe and Responsible Internet Use
474 W. Twenty-Ninth Ave.
Eugene, OR 97405
phone: (541) 556-1145
e-mail: contact@csriu.org • website: www.cyberbully.org

The Center for Safe and Responsible Internet Use works to help young people keep themselves safe and respect others on the Internet. Its website has numerous reports and guides designed to help people learn about responsible social networking behavior.

Common Sense Media
650 Townsend St., Suite 435
San Francisco, CA 94103
phone: (415) 863-0600 • fax: (415) 863-0601
website: www.commonsensemedia.org

Common Sense Media is an organization that believes all media have a profound influence on youth. It was created in order to help educate families about media, including social networking, and to give them the information and tools they need to make educated choices about their media use.

Electronic Frontier Foundation (EFF)
454 Shotwell St.
San Francisco, CA 94110
phone: (415) 436-9333
e-mail: information@eff.org • website: www.eff.org

The EFF is a nonprofit organization founded in 1990 that seeks to defend various civil liberties in relation to telecommunications technologies such as the Internet. Its website has information about free speech and privacy issues related to social networking.

GetNetWise
e-mail: cmatsuda@neted.org
website: www.getnetwise.org

GetNetWise is a website provided by Internet industry corporations and public interest organizations. Its goal is to ensure that Internet users have safe and constructive online experiences. The website contains information for both youth and parents about social networking, youth safety, security, and privacy.

Internet Society (ISOC)
1775 Wiehle Ave., Suite 201
Reston, VA 20190
phone: (703) 439-2120 • fax: (703) 326-9881
e-mail: isoc@isoc.org • website: www.internetsociety.org

The ISOC is an international nonprofit group that works to ensure the open development of the Internet for the benefit of people throughout the world. Its website contains information about social networking and privacy issues.

Media Smarts
950 Gladstone Ave., Suite 120
Ottawa, ON
Canada K1Y 3E6
phone: (613) 224-7721 • fax: (613) 761-9024
e-mail: info@mediasmarts.ca • website: http://mediasmarts.ca

Media Smarts is a Canadian organization that works to educate young people so that they can develop critical-thinking skills and be informed media users. Its website contains news, research, and articles about Internet use.

reSTART Internet and Technology Addiction Recovery
1001 290th Ave. SE
Fall City, WA 98024
phone: (800) 682-6934 • fax: (888) 788-3419
e-mail: contactus@NetAddictionRecovery.com
website: www.netaddictionrecovery.com

reSTART is a treatment facility whose mission is to help youths and adults recover from Internet and technology addiction. Its website features news articles, personal stories, and other information about addiction to social networking and other online activities.

Books

danah boyd, *It's Complicated: The Social Lives of Networked Teens*. New Haven, CT: Yale University Press, 2014.

Christian Fuchs, *Social Media: A Critical Introduction*. Los Angeles: Sage, 2014.

Alex Soojung-Kim Pang, *The Distraction Addiction: Getting the Information You Need and the Communication You Want, Without Enraging Your Family, Annoying Your Colleagues, and Destroying Your Soul*. New York: Little, Brown, 2013.

Catherine Steiner-Adair with Teresa H. Barker, *The Big Disconnect: Protecting Childhood and Family Relationships in the Digital Age*. New York: HarperCollins, 2013.

James P. Steyer, *Talking Back to Facebook: The Common Sense Guide to Raising Kids in the Digital Age*. New York: Scribner, 2012.

Internet Sources

American Press Institute, "How Millennials Get News: Inside the Habits of America's First Digital Generation," March 16, 2015. www.americanpressinstitute.org/publications/reports/survey-research/millennials-news.

Common Sense Media, "The Common Sense Census: Media Use by Tweens and Teens," 2015. www.commonsensemedia.org/sites/default/files/uploads/research/census_researchreport.pdf.

Simon Kemp, "Digital in 2016," We Are Social, January 27, 2016. http://wearesocial.com/special-reports/digital-in-2016.

Privacy Rights Clearinghouse, "Fact Sheet 35: Social Networking Privacy: How to Be Safe, Secure and Social," February 2016. www.privacyrights.org/social-networking-privacy-how-be-safe-secure-and-social.

Lee Rainie, "The State of Privacy in America: What We Learned," Pew Research Center, January 20, 2016. www.pewresearch.org/fact-tank/2016/01/20/the-state-of-privacy-in-america.

Websites

Cyberbullying Research Center (www.cyberbullying.us). This website is a collection of information about bullying on social networks and digital media. It contains information about the extent, causes, and consequences of this behavior, including personal stories from young people.

Reuters Institute Digital News Report (www.digitalnewsreport. org). This website contains research about the way people access news online. There are essays and data from an annual survey about digital news trends.

WiredSafety (www.wiredsafety.com). WiredSafety provides information about potential threats posed by social networking and includes information about how young people can protect themselves from these threats.

PICTURE CREDITS

Andrea C. Nakaya, a native of New Zealand, holds a BA in English and an MA in communications from San Diego State University. She has written and edited more than forty books on current issues. She currently lives in Encinitas, California, with her husband and their two children, Natalie and Shane.